Canoeing

By Laura Purdie Salas

Consultant:
Kevin Callan
Canoeist and Environmental Issues Instructor
Member, Canadian Recreational
Canoeing Association

CAPSTONE
HIGH-INTEREST
BOOKS

an imprint of Capstone Press
Mankato, Minnesota

797.1

Capstone High-Interest Books are published by Capstone Press
151 Good Counsel Drive, P.O. Box 669, Mankato, Minnesota 56002
http://www.capstone-press.com

Library of Congress Cataloging-in-Publication Data
Salas, Laura Purdie.
    Canoeing/by Laura P. Salas.
    p. cm.—(The great outdoors)
    Includes bibliographical references and index.
    Summary: Discusses the equipment, techniques, safety measures, and more
related to canoeing.
    ISBN 0-7368-1055-2
    1. Canoes and canoeing—Juvenile literature. [1. Canoes and canoeing.]
I. Title. II. Series.
GV784.3 .S25 2002
797.1'22—dc21
                                                          2001002855

Editorial Credits
Carrie Braulick, editor; Timothy Halldin, cover and interior designer; Katy Kudela,
    photo researcher

Photo Credits
Capstone Press/Gary Sundermeyer, cover (bottom left, bottom right), 4, 10, 12,
    18 (foreground), 20, 23 (foreground), 24, 27, 28, 30, 34, 41, 42 (all)
Comstock, Inc., 1, 18 (background), 23 (background)
Larry Prosor, cover (top right), 36
North Wind Picture Archives, 7
Photo Network/Morry Zipper, 38
Richard Hamilton Smith, 8, 14, 17

1 2 3 4 5 6 07 06 05 04 03 02

Table of Contents

CHAPTER 1

Canoeing

Canoeing can mean a relaxing float on a lake or an exciting trip down a fast-flowing river. It is a popular activity in North America. Some canoeists even spend several days on canoeing trips.

History of Canoeing

American Indians invented canoes thousands of years ago. They built these long, narrow boats from wood and animal skins. Each American Indian tribe built slightly different canoes. Some canoes fit just one person. Other canoes carried many people. Some of the large canoes were nearly 40 feet (12 meters) long.

During the 1500s and 1600s, European explorers arrived in North America. They crossed the Atlantic Ocean on large ships. But

Canoeing is a popular activity in North America.

these ships were too large for many North American waterways. The explorers used canoes to travel through these narrow passages.

During the 1700s, many settlers living in the northern United States and Canada traded furs for profit. People called voyageurs carried furs in large canoes to and from distant locations.

In the late 1800s, people became interested in using canoes for recreation. In the late 1850s, many North Americans began to experiment with canoe designs. Some people made lightweight canoes. Others experimented with different wood types.

Scottish lawyer John MacGregor encouraged people to canoe for recreation. In 1865, MacGregor designed a wooden canoe called "Rob Roy." It was 15 feet (4.6 meters) long. MacGregor paddled the canoe on long voyages throughout Europe. MacGregor then began to sell canoes similar to "Rob Roy." He formed a canoe club in Great Britain. He also wrote books and magazine articles about canoeing. Interest in the activity soon spread to North America.

Early North American settlers and American Indians often used canoes to transport furs.

Canoeing Today

Today, people canoe for various reasons. Some canoeists enjoy spending time outdoors. Many people use canoes to travel to camping locations. Some canoeists race in competitions.

North America offers many canoeing locations. Some people canoe on lakes or rivers. People also canoe on oceans or in water storage areas called reservoirs.

Whitewater canoeists paddle down river sections called rapids. These areas have strong currents that cause water to flow quickly. Rocks often are located close to the water's surface in rapids. Some rapids include small waterfalls.

North Americans can enjoy canoeing throughout much of the year. Most people canoe during the warm seasons of spring and summer. People also can enjoy canoeing during fall. People even can canoe during winter in the southern United States.

Whitewater canoeists paddle through river rapids.

CHAPTER 2

Equipment

Canoeists' basic equipment includes a canoe and paddles. But canoeists also need additional equipment to stay safe and comfortable.

The Canoe

Canoes can be made from a variety of materials. These materials include wood, plastic, and a lightweight metal called aluminum. They also may be made of fiberglass. This strong, lightweight material is made of woven glass fibers. Some canoes are made of a strong fiber called Kevlar.

Many canoes are made from a combination of materials. For example, canoes made of Royalex or Oltonar include foam, vinyl, and plastic.

Canoeists need a variety of equipment.

Canoeists often use recreational canoes on calm, smooth water.

All canoes have a similar type of design. The rounded body of the boat is called the hull. The bow is the hull's front. The stern is the hull's back. The gunwales are the upper edges of a canoe's sides.

Some canoes have a keel underneath them. This beam runs lengthwise across the canoe's center. A keel helps the canoe move in a straight line.

Thwarts stretch across the canoe's open top. These bars support the canoe. Most canoes have two to four thwarts.

People may choose different canoe designs depending on where they plan to canoe. People often use recreational canoes in lakes and other bodies of water that have little current. These canoes are about 16 to 18 feet (4.9 to 5.5 meters) long. The length helps the canoes travel quickly. River canoeists often use shorter canoes that are about 14 to 16 feet (4.3 to 4.9 meters) long.

River canoeists often use slightly rockered canoes. These boats have a curved bottom. Rockered canoes can turn quickly. They help canoeists avoid rocks and other obstacles in the water.

Whitewater canoeists often choose strong plastic canoes. The canoes usually are highly rockered to help the canoeists turn. Whitewater canoes have no keel. Canoeists often need to turn quickly in rapids. A keel can make the canoe difficult to turn.

Paddle parts include the grip, shaft, and blade.

Paddles

All canoe paddles have a similar design.
The grip is the paddle's top. It is rounded or
shaped like a "T." The shaft is the paddle's
long, narrow section. The blade is the wide,
rounded, or squared-off bottom.

Canoeists can choose from a variety of
paddles. Wooden paddles are ideal in a wide

variety of water conditions. Some canoeists choose paddles made of sassafras wood. This wood does not allow water to soak into its grain. Sassafras paddles often last several years without rotting.

Many canoeists in open areas without currents use bent-shaft paddles. These paddles are bent just above the blade. They help canoeists gain speed and require less effort to move the canoe than other paddles.

Whitewater canoeists often use lightweight paddles made of materials such as plastic or aluminum. These paddles are more durable than many other paddles.

Life Jackets

Canoeists need to wear a life jacket to keep them afloat if they fall into the water. Many states and provinces have laws that require people in boats to wear a life jacket at all times.

Canoeists often wear Type III life jackets approved by the U.S. Coast Guard. The U.S. Coast Guard inspects the design of these jackets. Type III life jackets look similar to vests. These life jackets are less bulky than many other styles. They help canoeists paddle comfortably.

Life jackets should fit securely. They should only rise about 2 inches (5 centimeters) when canoeists pull them up.

Clothing

Canoeists often dress in layers. They then can add and remove clothing as the weather changes. Canoeists often wear synthetic fabrics for the first layer. These materials are made by people. Some canoeists wear a lightweight, warm fabric called polypropylene for the first layer. This material dries quickly.

Canoeists may choose fleece or wool for the second layer. Fleece is soft, warm, and breathable. It allows moisture to pass through to the outer layers. Wool keeps canoeists warm even after it becomes wet.

Canoeists must wear life jackets that fit comfortably and securely.

The final layer is called the shell. Many canoeists wear a strong material called nylon for the shell. Nylon is resistant to wind and water. Canoeists also may choose a synthetic fabric called Gore-Tex. This breathable material has a water-repellent finish.

Peanut Butter Treats

Ingredients:
½ cup (125 mL) peanut butter
½ cup (125 mL) granola
½ cup (125 mL) honey
⅓ cup (75 mL) powdered
  milk
¼ cup (50 mL) miniature chocolate
  chips

Equipment:
Large bowl
Mixing spoon
Plastic container

1. Mix all of the ingredients together in bowl with spoon.

2. Roll the mixture into balls about the size of golf balls.

3. Store peanut butter treats in plastic container.

Makes 16 to 18 treats

Canoeists should not wear cotton clothing such as jeans. Cotton dries slowly. It can chill canoeists and make them uncomfortable.

Canoeists need proper footwear. Their shoes should protect their feet from objects such as sharp rocks. Canoeists walk in the water to enter and exit their canoes. Many canoeists wear water shoes because they dry quickly. These shoes often are made of nylon mesh or a synthetic rubber material called neoprene.

Other Items

Canoeists need other items. They should have a detailed map of the area to help them stay on course. Many canoeists bring a canoe repair kit. This kit often includes items such as a pliers, wire, and duct tape. Canoeists should have a bailer. They can use this container to scoop water out of their canoes. Canoeists also should have a whistle in case of an emergency. They can blow the whistle to alert others.

Canoeists should bring high-energy food on their trips.

Canoeists should bring sunscreen and sunglasses to protect their skin and eyes from the sun. They also should bring high-energy snacks such as beef jerky, fruit, or peanuts. Each canoeist should have at least 2 quarts (1.9 liters) of drinking water for each day of the trip.

Canoeists also carry throw ropes. These ropes are filled with foam. The foam makes the ropes float on the water's surface. Canoeists can use throw ropes to rescue someone who has fallen into the water.

Canoeists who plan to camp need camping equipment. These items may include a tent, sleeping bag, and a small cooking stove. Canoeists who camp also need extra food, drinking water, and clothing.

All canoeists should carry first aid kits. These kits usually include aspirin, tweezers, and scissors. They also include adhesive bandages and gauze pads to cover wounds. First aid kits often have antibacterial cream or spray to protect wounds from germs.

River Canoeing Equipment
River canoeists need extra items. They usually place waterproof bags called float bags at each

end of their canoes. These bags are filled with air. They help a canoe stay afloat if it capsizes. A canoe that capsizes tips over in the water.

River canoeists also tie polypropylene ropes called painters to each end of their canoes. These ropes usually are about 6 to 10 feet (1.8 to 3 meters) long. After a canoe capsizes, canoeists can grab a painter to prevent the boat from floating away.

Equipment

- Bailer
- Drinking water
- First aid kit
- Float bags
- High-energy snacks
- Life jacket
- Map
- Paddles
- Repair kit
- Sunglasses
- Sunscreen
- Throw rope
- Whistle

CHAPTER 3

Skills and Techniques

Canoeists must know how to prepare for their trip and be able to paddle and steer their canoe. Two people usually canoe together. It is easier for tandem canoeists to steer a canoe than it is for one person.

Planning a Canoe Trip

Canoeists should carefully plan their trip. They must decide the trip's length. Beginning canoeists usually take short trips that begin and end the same day. They also may take short camping trips of one or two days.

Canoeists need to choose a canoeing area that fits their skill level. Beginning canoeists

Canoeists should carefully plan their route before they begin their trip.

should canoe in calm water without currents. These areas include lakes, ponds, and marshes. Most rivers have currents that can make controlling a canoe difficult. Only skilled canoeists should canoe in rivers.

Portaging

Canoeists should know how to properly portage canoes. Canoeists carry canoes when they portage. They may need to portage their canoes between water areas or from their vehicle to a water area.

One person usually portages a canoe. This canoeist should turn the canoe upside down and rest it on the shoulders. Some canoes have a yoke. This piece of padding fits around a canoeist's shoulders. It helps canoeists portage comfortably.

Two people may portage a canoe for very short distances. One person holds the canoe's bow. The other person holds the canoe's stern. They walk on opposite sides of the canoe.

One person usually portages a canoe.

Getting Started

Canoeists should stretch to warm up their muscles before they begin canoeing. This activity helps canoeists prevent injuries. They should stretch the waist, neck, back, shoulders, and arms.

One person should steady a canoe while the other person enters it.

Canoeists follow several steps as they enter the boat. They first place the canoe in shallow water. One person holds the canoe's stern. The other person holds onto the boat's gunwales and enters its middle from the side. The person steadying the canoe then gently enters the boat's stern. Both canoeists keep their bodies low to prevent the boat from capsizing.

Paddling Position

Canoeists hold the paddle in the same way for most strokes. They place one hand on top of the grip with their knuckles pointing upward. This hand is called the grip hand. They place the other hand on the shaft just above the blade. This hand is called the shaft hand.

Canoeists can use different paddling positions. They often kneel on the canoe's bottom as they paddle. This position keeps the canoe steady.

Canoeists sometimes sit on the canoe's seats to rest their knees. But this position makes canoes less stable. A seated position raises the canoe's center of gravity. A canoe stays most stable when the center of gravity is near the canoe's bottom. Canoeists should sit only in calm water.

Advanced canoeists sometimes stand to see what is ahead of them. But this position makes the canoe most likely to capsize.

The bow and stern canoeist work together to move the canoe forward. The stern canoeist usually steers and keeps the boat moving in a straight line. The bow canoeist sometimes helps the stern canoeist steer.

The stern canoeist makes correction strokes to steer a canoe.

In whitewater canoeing, the bow canoeist usually steers. Bow canoeists can see obstacles sooner than stern canoeists. They then can steer around the obstacles.

Forward Stroke
The forward stroke is the most common stroke. This stroke also is called the power stroke. It moves the boat forward.

The bow and stern canoeists paddle from opposite sides to perform the forward stroke. They move the shaft hand forward. They then move the grip hand forward. Canoeists place the blade underwater and move the paddle back. This movement pushes the canoe forward. They stop the backward movement as the blade passes their knees.

Correction Strokes

The canoe sometimes does not move forward in a straight line. The stern canoeist then uses correction strokes. The most common correction strokes are the J-stroke and the stern pry.

The stern canoeist begins the J-stroke with a forward stroke. The wrist of the grip hand twists when the paddle comes alongside the canoeist's hip. The grip hand's thumb should rotate downward or away from the body. The canoeist also turns the shaft hand toward the body. The canoeist then slightly pushes the paddle away from the boat. The paddle makes a "J" shape in the water.

The stern pry is similar to the J-stroke. But it is more powerful than the J-stroke. The stern pry

Eddies

Canoeists must understand eddies. An eddy is an area of water that flows upstream instead of downstream. The boundary between the water flowing downstream and the water flowing upstream is called an eddy line. Structures and obstacles in the water such as rocks and logs can cause an eddy. An eddy can trap a canoe or person between the obstacle and the upstream current. An eddy also may cause a canoe to capsize.

Canoeists sometimes rest their canoes in eddies. These canoeists should be careful as they enter eddies. An eddy's upstream current can pull on the bottom of the boat and cause it to capsize.

Canoeists also can safely move around eddies. The downstream current forms a "V" shape around eddies. Canoeists can angle their boats away from an eddy. They then can follow the downstream current around it.

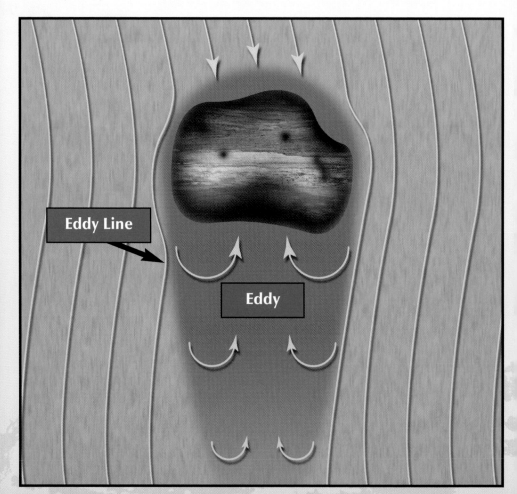

begins with a forward stroke. The canoeist places the blade in the water and slides the paddle's shaft back along the gunwale. The canoeist turns the grip hand's wrist so the thumb points upward as the paddle comes alongside the body. The canoeist then pulls the grip toward the boat. This action turns the canoe.

Other Strokes

The sweep stroke allows canoeists to move in a circle. One of the canoeists places the blade in the water. This canoeist then moves the blade in a wide arc toward the closest end of the canoe.

The draw stroke moves the canoe sideways. One canoeist places the blade in the water far out to one side of the canoe. The canoeist then brings the shaft hand straight toward the canoe. This action causes the boat to move sideways toward the paddle. The canoe moves in a circle when both canoeists perform a draw stroke from opposite sides.

CHAPTER 4

Conservation

Canoeists should take care of the environment. Responsible canoeists do not pollute water sources or land areas. They deal with trash responsibly. They choose camping areas that will not damage the environment. Some canoeists join groups to clean polluted areas.

Water Pollution

Many of North America's water sources are polluted. Farmers often use chemicals to help their crops grow. These chemicals can pollute water sources. Wastes from factories and other businesses also can pollute water sources. Pollutants can enter the bodies of fish. These fish can become sick or die. Pollutants also can make water sources unsafe for swimming.

Responsible canoeists pick up trash left by others.

Canoeists should enter and exit the water near level ground.

Responsible canoeists enter and exit the water near level ground. This practice helps prevent soil erosion. Soil that wears away in steep areas can easily enter a water source. A great deal of soil in water sources can cause flooding. It also can damage areas where fish lay eggs.

Some groups try to clean polluted water sources or prevent water pollution. Government agencies such as the U.S. Fish and Wildlife

Service and Environment Canada often create programs to improve water sources. They may plant trees and shrubs along waterways to prevent pollutants from entering the water. They also may use large machines to dredge water sources that contain a large amount of soil. The machines dig the soil out of the water.

Camping

Canoeists who want to camp should choose their campsites responsibly. They should camp at campgrounds or other established locations. Established campsites may have running water and places for campers to make a campfire.

Campers should set up campsites in rocky or sandy areas in non-established locations. This practice helps prevent damage to plants.

Campers should try to leave their campsite exactly the way they found it. They should return any sticks, rocks, or other items to their original locations. Campers should put trash in a trash can or place it in a plastic bag. They can throw away the trash when they return home.

CHAPTER 5

Safety

Canoeists must stay safe both inside and outside of their canoes. They should always wear life jackets while canoeing. They should be aware of the weather forecast. Canoeists also should have rescue skills.

Weather Safety

Canoeists should check the weather forecast before they begin their trip. They should not canoe if storms are likely. Some canoeists check the Beaufort Scale before their trip. This scale rates wind speeds from 1 to 12. At force 1, the wind speed is between 1 and 3 miles (1.6 and 4.8 kilometers) per hour. The water is flat and calm. At force 12, hurricane-like winds can cause a great deal of damage to buildings

The water is calm when wind speeds are low.

and other structures. The wind speed is at least 75 miles (121 kilometers) per hour.

Canoeists should not canoe in winds that rate higher than force 5 on the Beaufort Scale. The wind speed at this level is between 19 and 24 miles (31 and 39 kilometers) per hour. Winds stronger than force 5 can cause canoes to capsize. The wind also can form large waves. The waves can cause a great deal of water to enter canoes.

People who are canoeing when a storm occurs should paddle toward shore. Water easily carries electricity. Canoeists who are on the water when lightning strikes may get a shock.

Rescues

Canoeists sometimes fall out of their canoes. These canoeists sometimes can swim to safety. But they may need to be rescued.

Other canoeists can paddle out to someone who has capsized. They then can toss a painter rope or a throw rope to the victim. Rescuers

Canoeists may use a throw rope to rescue someone who has capsized.

then tow the capsized canoeist to shore. In a river, rescuers should move downstream of the capsized person.

People on shore also can toss a throw rope to a canoeist in the water. The rescuers then can pull the canoeist to shore.

Canoeing River Signals

Canoeists can use river signals to communicate with others. These signals help keep canoeists safe on rivers.

Stop

Canoeists use this signal if they want other canoeists to stop. They hold the paddle to form a "T." They then outstretch their arms above their head.

Help/Emergency

Canoeists make this signal if they need help. The canoeists give three long whistle blasts and wave a paddle, helmet, or life jacket over their head.

All Clear

This signal tells other canoeists to come ahead. Canoeists hold their hand or paddle straight up to tell others to move down the route's center. Canoeists hold their hand or paddle at an angle to tell others to follow a route to the side. Canoeists point in the direction they want people to go if there is a structure to avoid.

Whitewater Safety

Whitewater canoeists use equipment to help keep themselves safe. They wear helmets in case they fall out of their canoes. They place at least two float bags in their canoes. The bags help the canoes float high on the water's surface. This position prevents the canoes from scraping rocks.

Canoeists should choose rapids based on their skill level. Beginning whitewater canoeists should choose rapids with small waves and few obstacles. Advanced whitewater canoeists may choose rapids with large waves and a great deal of obstacles.

Other Safety Guidelines

Canoeists should follow other safety guidelines. They should be able to identify harmful plants such as poison ivy, poison oak, and poison sumac. These plants can cause a skin rash. Canoeists should have basic first aid skills to treat people who become injured.

Responsible canoeists follow safety guidelines and have good rescue skills. These canoeists can help make their sport safer and set a good example for other canoeists.

Words to Know

capsize (KAP-size)—to tip over in the water

erode (i-RODE)—to wear away; soil in a steep area can erode and enter a water source.

gunwale (GUHN-wayl)—the upper edge of a canoe's side

keel (KEEL)—a long beam that runs lengthwise across the bottom of some canoes; a keel helps keep a canoe moving in a straight line.

portage (POOR-tij)—to carry a canoe

rapids (RAP-idz)—a rocky section of a river with quickly flowing water; whitewater canoeists travel in rapids.

shaft (SHAFT)—the long, narrow section of a paddle

thwart (THWORT)—a bar that stretches across the top of a canoe

To Learn More

Cooper, Jason. *Canoes and Kayaks.* Boats and Ships. Vero Beach, Fla.: Rourke, 1999.

Ditchfield, Christin. *Kayaking, Canoeing, Rowing, and Yachting.* A True Book. New York: Children's Press, 2000.

Page, Jason. *On the Water: Rowing, Yachting, Canoeing, and Lots, Lots More.* Zeke's Olympic Pocket Guide. Minneapolis: LernerSports, 2000.

Useful Addresses

American Canoe Association
7432 Alban Station Boulevard
Suite B-232
Springfield, VA 22150

Canadian Recreational Canoeing Association
446 Main Street West
Merrickville, ON K0G 1N0
Canada

National Park Service
1849 C Street NW
Washington, DC 20240

Internet Sites

American Canoe Association
http://www.acanet.org/acanet.htm

Canadian Recreational Canoeing Association
http://www.crca.ca/crcacore.cfm

Great Outdoor Recreation Pages—Paddling
http://www.gorp.com/gorp/activity/paddle.htm

National Park Service
http://www.nps.gov

REI Learn & Share—Paddling
http://www.rei.com/reihtml/LEARN_SHARE/
index.jsp?ls=Paddling

Index